LITTLE QUICK FIX:

GET YOUR DATA FROM SOCIAL MEDIA

#LittleQuickFix

LITTLE QUICK FIX:

GET YOUR DATA FROM SOCIAL MEDIA

Nicola Thomas

Los Angeles | London | New Delhi
Singapore | Washington DC | Melbourne

Los Angeles | London | New Delhi
Singapore | Washington DC | Melbourne

SAGE Publications Ltd
1 Oliver's Yard
55 City Road
London EC1Y 1SP

SAGE Publications Inc.
2455 Teller Road
Thousand Oaks, California 91320

SAGE Publications India Pvt Ltd
B 1/I 1 Mohan Cooperative Industrial Area
Mathura Road
New Delhi 110 044

SAGE Publications Asia-Pacific Pte Ltd
3 Church Street
#10-04 Samsung Hub
Singapore 049483

© Nicola Thomas 2020

First published 2020

Editor: Alysha Owen
Editorial assistant: Lauren Jacobs
Production editor: Katherine Haw
Proofreader: Clare Weaver
Marketing manager: Ben Sherwood
Cover design: Lisa Harper-Wells
Typeset by: C&M Digitals (P) Ltd, Chennai, India
Printed in the UK

Library of Congress Control Number: 2019950158

British Library Cataloguing in Publication data

A catalogue record for this book is available
from the British Library

ISBN 978-1-5297-0970-4

At SAGE we take sustainability seriously. Most of our products are printed in the UK using responsibly
sourced papers and boards. When we print overseas we ensure sustainable papers are used as measured
by the PREPS grading system. We undertake an annual audit to monitor our sustainability.

Contents

2 MIN summary

Everything in this book!

Section 1 Social media data can serve many research needs. It is important to know the potential, and pitfalls, of social media data. Decide how social media data can provide a good fit for your research.

Section 2 Conduct your social media research to high ethical standards. Understand and address ethical dilemmas when obtaining and using social media data.

Section 3 Choose the type and scope of social media data. Decide what type of data you need, from where, when and from whom or what, to decide the best approach.

Section 4 Develop a robust sampling strategy to obtain social media data. Identify your population, sampling frame, sample and sampling technique(s) to best meet your research needs.

Section 5 There are three ways to extract social media data. Know how to extract social media data, either manually, computationally, or a hybrid approach, to best suit your research needs, capabilities and resources.

Section 6 Take strategic steps to plan your data collection. Thinking through, and planning out, your data collection will increase your chances of generating valuable insights from your social media data.

**Social media data
can serve many
research needs**

Section

1

Can social media data meet my research needs?

summary

Social media data can shed
light on a huge variety of social
phenomena. It can serve many
research needs, but it's important
to understand its limitations.

Social media research is diverse, dynamic and challenging

The enormous popularity of social media platforms and the digital means to generate, share and consume content, and socially interact, leave rich digital traces that can be used for research. Data enable us to describe, explain, predict and evaluate a huge range of online and offline social phenomena. But **as with all data types, social media data does have limitations.**

DEFINING SOCIAL MEDIA DATA

Social media data is an umbrella term for the different kinds of digital traces produced by or about social media users. A huge volume of data emerges from real-time social interactions on a variety of online and mobile social media platforms. For instance, some platforms offer opportunities for social networking (e.g. Facebook), questions and answers (e.g. Quora), reviewing (e.g. TripAdvisor), image and video sharing (e.g. Instagram), instant messaging (e.g. WhatsApp), collaboration (e.g. Wikipedia), gamifying mobile check-ins (e.g. FourSquare), expressing deeper thoughts (e.g. Medium) and sharing economies (e.g. AirBnb).

THE RESEARCH VALUE OF SOCIAL MEDIA DATA

Collectively, social media platforms create an interactive social web where billions of people come together to generate, share and consume content. The sheer volume, velocity and variety of social media data therefore presents a valuable opportunity to conduct research.

HUGE NUMBER OF RESEARCH TOPICS

There is no shortage of research topics. Given the massive amount of social media data generated by individuals, communities and organizations, we could choose from any number of topics – from consumer choices, disease outbreaks – to policy interventions. Social media data are now widely used in the social sciences. It doesn't matter whether you are studying psychology, anthropology or sociology, medical or political science, human geography or business, it's very likely your discipline has already found genuine research value in using social media data.

YOUR RESEARCH NEEDS WILL GUIDE YOU

Given the daunting range of social phenomena potentially available to research, it's best to start with your own research needs. Which topic ignites a passion in you? What problem do you want to solve? What will your theoretical contribution be? What is your research question? If you're currently unsure, the following sections will help you decide.

DATA FOR DIFFERENT AIMS

We can use social media data for different research purposes. Do you want to describe, explain, predict or evaluate something? Below are some real-world examples of how social media data are being put to different uses:

Description: What is happening?

Understanding negative word-of-mouth dynamics in social media networks.

Explanation: Why is this happening?

The role of psychological traits in explaining Facebook use.

Prediction: What will happen in the future?

Forecasting stock market fluctuations.

Evaluation: Did it work?

Assessing social networking interventions to treat depression in young people.

THREE CROSS-CUTTING TYPES

Social media research tends to fall into three broad types.

1. **Online phenomena** Researching social phenomena manifested in social media environments. For instance, how people construct online identities, or how they think, feel and behave.

2. **Offline phenomena** To understand real-world events. For instance, by investigating the spread of diseases by analysing online reported symptoms.

3. **Platform phenomena** Looking at how social media platform(s) shape and influence people, for instance, due to their design functionality.

A RICH VARIETY OF METHODS

Social media data are amenable to an increasing number of data collection and analytical methods. Below are some popular choices.

Quantitative methods

- Quantitative content analysis
- Data mining
- Social network analysis
- Natural Language Processing
- Visual analytics

Qualitative

- Qualitative content analysis

- Discourse analysis

- Netnography

- Online ethnography

- Online focus groups

Tip: Consult contemporary sources as methods are increasingly being developed, advanced and adapted for social media contexts.

KNOW YOUR DATA
LIMITATIONS

Social media presents a significant research opportunity. However, we must be mindful of its pitfalls.

Shrinking data access. Many social media platforms allow data access. However, data accessed via application programming interfaces (APIs) are curated and data availability is shrinking. People often refer to the massive stream of social media data as the firehose. For most of us, the firehose is out of reach. The accessible portion resembles a garden hose (10%) or a sprinkler (1%).

Missing metadata. While profiles can be data rich, users are not required to publish demographic data. Without knowing who users are, attempts to understand how a phenomenon relates to age, gender, class, and so on, can be undermined.

Disproportionate representation. Social media populations do not represent human populations. For instance, the Twitter population overrepresents males, and underrepresents older cohorts. Neither should we assume the types of users on one platform are the same as another.

Identity play. People can present and express themselves differently in online and offline contexts. This can call the authenticity of our data into question.

Beware social bots. Non-human agents are prevalent on social media. Spot and remove them from your dataset … unless they are the topic of your research!

EVERY CLOUD HAS A SILVER LINING

Most researchers are in the same boat. Even fully established and well-funded researchers face the same pitfalls. You are not alone.

Honesty is a virtue. Demonstrating that you recognize and understand these types of research limitations and bias will be looked upon favourably.

Every problem is an opportunity. Research is increasingly attempting to understand and overcome these limitations. Perhaps you could too.

THE PROS + CONS OF SOCIAL MEDIA DATA

CHECKPOINT

Answer the questions below

1 What is social media data?

....

....

....

2 What four research aims can be met using social media data?

1 ....

2 ....

3 ....

4 ....

3 It is difficult to access large representative datasets. **True / False**

23

2

Section

Conduct your social media research to high ethical standards

How do I gather and use social media data ethically?

summary

You need to address ethical guidelines and
legalities, privacy and consent, as well as
minimize potential risk of harm to participants.

Be ethical!

Before getting your social media data, it is essential to **think through, and address, a range of ethical issues**. Each stage of your social media research plan has its own distinct challenges. You need to consider your data source(s), target population, sampling strategy, and how you extract, store and use your data.

THE FOUR GOLDEN RULES OF ETHICAL RESEARCH

Ethical research adheres to four golden rules:

1 do good

2 do no harm

3 be respectful

4 treat people fairly

There are currently no 'hard and fast' rules on how to best apply these golden rules in social media research. The best advice is to err on the side of caution. To help you do this, this section provides guidance on how to address the ethical dilemmas raised by working with social media data. At the very least, and if in any doubt, always consult your institution's ethics guidelines and those of your discipline.

START WITH YOUR
DATA SOURCE

Check legal terms. Social media platforms provide terms for use and privacy. It is important you consult these terms to make sure the access and data you want is permitted. As terms change, make yourself familiar with the most current version to prevent you from violating any conditions.

BE AWARE OF SOCIAL MEDIA AGREEMENTS

Let's assume you are a regular social media user. How often have you read these terms? Like others, you may have skipped the reading bit and hastily clicked your agreement. In fact, you may have agreed to things that you didn't even realize! Due to this thorny issue, some people think that informed consent is a must, even if the data are publicly available. To help navigate this issue within ethical bounds, most researchers first consider whether the data they wish to collect is really public.

KNOW IF YOUR DATA IS REALLY PUBLIC

Is the data you want really public? The big question you need to answer is: Would the social media user(s) you wish to collect data from reasonably expect to be observed by you? To help answer this big question, let's break it down into three smaller questions.

1   Is the data you wish to gather from an open platform, such as Twitter?

2   Does the platform allow the user to control the amount of data that is publicly available, such as protected Tweets and direct messages?

3   Does the data you need already exist? In other words, has the data already been user generated, rather than elicited directly by you, such as by asking interview or survey questions?

If you answered yes to these three questions, then you could consider the data as public.

THE NEED FOR INFORMED CONSENT

Alternatively, you may want to get data from private sources that require permission.

1   Is your data located within a private forum, for example a closed Facebook forum?

2   Is the data held within a password-protected space?

3   Is there a gatekeeper or administrator involved?

4   Will you be interacting with participants, for instance, by asking questions, to elicit new data?

If you answered yes to any of these questions, you must gain informed consent.

CONSIDER RISK OF VULNERABILITY

Regardless of whether your data are sourced from public or private spaces, user generated or elicited, it is essential you identify and respond to the level of risk your research could pose.

Are your research participants vulnerable? You have a responsibility to your participants. Potentially vulnerable people, for example children, older persons or adults with learning disabilities, need careful consideration. For instance, a vulnerable person may not have the ability to withdraw from an online interview, even if they feel uncomfortable. Nor can you necessarily rely on a participant's ability to provide informed consent. In the case of minors, you must always seek parental consent.

BE CAREFUL OF
THE UNKNOWN

Identity, age and capabilities can be unknown or hidden. For example, a young child may pretend to be older than they are. This means it is often difficult to infer vulnerability. Given this challenge, it's important to think and plan ahead. What could you do to minimize any potential harm?

IS YOUR DATA SENSITIVE?

It's ultimately up to you, and your institution, to decide whether your data could be sensitive. Here are some pointers to help you decide.

According to the European Union, 'sensitive' personal data covers:

- personal data revealing racial or ethnic origin

- political opinions, religious or philosophical beliefs

- trade union membership

- genetic data, biometric data processed solely to identify a human being

- health-related data; and data concerning a person's sex life or sexual orientation.

If your data falls into any of these categories, you can safely assume it's sensitive.

EVEN MUNDANE ACTIVITIES CAN CAUSE HARM

If the data you want concerns everyday stuff, like recipes, the weather or fashion, it's unlikely to contain sensitive information. Yet even mundane information can cause harm. For instance, if data are taken out of context and/or exposed to new audiences, it could lead to emotional distress and reputational damage. As such, it's important to consider how your data will be used, now and in the future.

CONSENT MATTERS

Informed consent is required if you want to directly elicit data, access data from private online spaces, if your topic is sensitive and/or participants are vulnerable. You will also need permission to reuse copyrighted materials, such as images, audio and video data. However, gaining informed consent when the desired dataset is large is problematic.

Realistically, gaining informed consent from hundreds or thousands of users may be too difficult, even impossible. Many researchers bypass the informed consent step, but only if their data are considered public. Regardless, there are several more steps that researchers should take to avoid harm to participants.

RESPECT ANONYMITY

Remove all identifiable features, including user handles and profile pictures, from your dataset. Exceptions are made however for data generated by public figures or organizations, such as celebrities, campaigners or brands, as posts are intended to be shared widely.

In the case where you are mapping geotagged social media data, and individuals could be potentially identified, you should also apply a 'geomask' to protect a person's privacy.

Be aware of a caveat. Some social media users may prefer to waive anonymity, preferring to take credit for their content.

STORE DATA SECURELY

All your data – raw and coded – must be kept safe, secure and protected. Password-protected devices, files and encryption are good options. Always consult your institution's guidelines as they may contain specific recommendations, including how long your data can be kept.

SHARE DATA WISELY

You may want to publish your data, for instance, at a conference or in a blogpost or article. Yet social media data extracts, such as Tweets, published verbatim, can be retraced back to their source. To prevent harm, consider three options:

1 aggregate data

2 gain consent from those users whose extracts you wish to publish, or

3 without losing context, paraphrase extracts to prevent identification.

HOW TO GET ETHICAL AUTHORIZATION

CHECKPOINT

Follow this checklist to make sure your social media research is ethical.

Legalities:

❑ Consult research ethics guidelines (e.g. institutional, disciplinary).

❑ Read platform terms for public data access and/or user contact.

❑ Seek permission to reuse copyrightable materials.

Privacy, risk and consent:

❑ Protect privacy and bring no harm to your research participants.

❑ Identify and address any risks, e.g. working with vulnerable people.

❑ Gain informed consent. Alternatively, explicitly state why informed consent is not possible and gain institutional authorization before data gathering.

Data storage, use and reuse:

❑ Secure all your data safely during and after your study.

❑ Anonymize your dataset to protect privacy and enable confidentiality.

❑ State how you will protect participants from harm if you publish data extracts.

**Choose the type and
scope of social media data**

Section

3

What social media data do I need?

A

summary

It will depend on the
phenomenon you want to
research and the question you
are trying to answer.

Get the data you need

With so much social media data created daily, it's sometimes difficult to know what data to choose. **Let your research needs guide you**. First, you need to check whether the data are a good fit for your research aims. You'll also need to figure out the 'who' or the 'what' you want to study, as well as where and when you will observe, measure or collect your data. Above all, let your research question help you choose the type and scope of social media data.

GET THE RIGHT
DATA FIT

Your data must match the scope of your research.

Micro-level data are used to study small-scale phenomena. This could be at the level of an individual, small-scale inter-personal interactions or a brand post.

Meso-level data looks at group-level phenomena. For instance, if you want to study an online community, then your data will be occurring at the meso level.

Macro-level data looks at large-scale phenomena. Macro data tend to occur at a network or population level.

Cross-level data looks at the relationship between two or more concepts that occur at different levels.

A HYPOTHETICAL EXAMPLE: CROSS-LEVEL RESEARCH

Let's imagine your research topic is the #MeToo movement, and you want to understand story flows between:

- friends involved in inter-personal communications (micro-level)

- expert and activist groups (meso-level) and

- mass media outlets and celebrities with 5M+ followings (macro-level).

By looking at the story flows between these three different levels, you would be embarking on a cross-level study.

UNITS OF ANALYSIS VS OBSERVATION

Unit of analysis is the 'who' or the 'what' you want to study. The unit of analysis will likely be people – consumers, voters, patients and so on – or cases – organizations, brands, political parties, cities – or objects – hashtags, posts, fan pages, platforms.

Don't confuse unit of analysis with unit of observation. A unit of observation is the data you will observe, measure or collect to understand your unit of analysis. If your unit of analysis is a person, your units of observation could be feelings, thoughts and behaviours.

Only when the data you want is the same as the entity you want to understand, is your unit of analysis the same as your unit of observation.

THE SOCIAL WEB IS A NESTED ENTITY

Your unit of analysis, whether it's the social web itself or an individual post, will contain many potential units of observation nested within it.

This is an abstract illustration and far from exhaustive! Start thinking now about your different types of units.

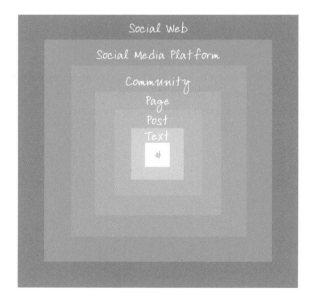

WILL YOUR RESEARCH BE BOUNDED AT THE PLATFORM LEVEL?

The scope of our research will also be potentially bounded at the platform level.

Here are some questions to ask yourself:

- Is your unit of analysis a platform? Will you choose one or more platforms?

- Does the online or offline phenomenon you are interested in studying manifest on a particular platform or several?

- Does your unit of analysis, such as a hashtag or group level activity, migrate across different platforms? Will you follow these cross-platform dynamics or bound your study to one platform?

- Can your units of observation (e.g. likes, hashtags, conversations) be easily compared at a cross-platform level? Do they behave the same or differently on different platforms?

- Do the cultural norms that govern practices on one platform differ from another?

Irrespective of your answers to these questions, you will need to justify how you bound your research at the platform level.

LOCATION, LOCATION, LOCATION

Whether or not your unit of analysis is a geographic location, most studies are geographically bounded. For instance, your target population could be UK Twitter users or a restaurant in Manchester. There are four ways to identify location:

1   Geo-tagged posts. These are available when a user opts in to share location. These tags have research value, but they represent a tiny fraction of posts... unless you're working with geographical check-ins, such as FourSquare data.

2   Explicit profile references. Users often state location in their profiles. This can be problematic. Is this location where they live, work or where they're originally from?

3 Semantic information. Users may post location information in their generated content. These direct semantic references, albeit less precise, can identify location.

4 Infer location. Location can be inferred indirectly from what people post. This could be place content in a photograph or a comment a user has made, e.g. "I'm just down the road from….".

The last three ways constitute proxy measures of geographic location. Researchers also use proxy measures for age, gender, occupation, class and language.

TIME MATTERS

As social media posts are time stamped, digital temporal traces can be mined for temporal insights. Temporal data can be cross-sectional, as in 'near time' or 'right now' snapshots or longitudinal, either retrospectively (in the past) or prospectively (as the future unfolds).

Thinking back to our hypothetical #MeToo example, that means we could look at anything from mood rhythms (micro) to movement dynamics (macro), from different temporal perspectives:

- The initial emergence of the #MeToo movement (retrospective longitudinal)

- The current dynamics of the #MeToo movement (cross-sectional)

- The future trajectory of the #MeToo movement (prospective longitudinal).

TIME
FLIES

If we opt for a longitudinal study, a study's duration, and choice of time units, will depend on what we're interested in studying.

Due to the quirky temporality of Snapchat, time units could be relatively small, such as in hours, even minutes. Alternatively, the dynamics inherent to natural disasters, disease outbreaks, political uprisings or corporate scandals, could play out over much longer time spans.

LET YOUR RESEARCH QUESTION GUIDE YOU

Your research question will contain strong clues as to what type and scope of social media data you will need to get.

Does your question …

- Concern people, cases or objects?

- Involve micro, meso, macro or cross-level phenomena?

- Mention any theoretical entities, such as variables, concepts, constructs or principles?

- Look for … a pattern, an effect, a relation, an occurrence, and so on?

- Concern a dimension … in the here and now, or over space and/or time?

Identify your unit of analysis.

Unit of Analysis ....

Which digital traces will form your units of observation?

Units of Observation

1 ....

2 ....

3 ....

4 ....

5 ....

6 ....

7 ....

ANSWERS

Possible Answers

Unit of Analysis – Social network ties

Possible observations: Similarities (location, membership, attributes); Social relations (roles, affective, cognitive); Interactions (helped, harmed, talked to, advice to); Flows (information, beliefs, people, resources).

Unit of Analysis – Social media posts

Possible observations: Content (text, photos, video, audio); Interactive elements (hashtag, links); Communication resources (emojis, emoticons); Engagement (likes, comments, replies).

And these are just a few suggested answers!

CONGRATULATIONS!

NOW YOU UNDERSTAND WHAT SOCIAL MEDIA DATA BEST FITS YOUR RESEARCH!

Develop a robust sampling strategy to obtain social media data

4

Section

How do I build an effective sampling strategy?

summary

By familiarizing yourself
with some basic
sampling principles
before getting your
social media data.

60
SEC
summary

Preparation is key

Cherry picking data can produce dubious results. **Putting together a sampling strategy will help you produce high-quality findings**. You need to consider your population of interest and sampling frame, your intended sample characteristics, as well as how you will select your sample.

SOCIAL MEDIA SAMPLING STRATEGY

An effective social media sampling strategy involves making several important decisions to make sure we produce high-quality findings.

- The population of units of analysis we are interested in researching.

- The sampling frame and our choice of sample and sample size.

- The potential for sampling bias and deciding whether or not it's important.

- The need to consider different sampling techniques.

UNDERSTANDING POPULATION

In sampling, a population is the complete set of units of analysis (people, cases or objects) that possess the characteristics we are interested in.

- University student Instagram active users

- Video game online communities

- Pinterest pins related to fashion consumption

- YouTube subscribers aged 65 years and over

- Top 5 UK Law firm followers on Twitter

- Food-related 'selfies' posted on Snapchat

Tip: Be specific. For instance, when we say 'active' users, we need to specify what we mean by 'active' (e.g. people who log-in at least once a day).

CONSTRUCTING A SAMPLING FRAME

A sampling frame is a complete list of our units of analysis – people, cases or objects – in our population. The population is general; the frame is specific. For example:

Population: Video game online communities

Sampling frame: NeoGAF, GameFAQS, Gamespot, and so on.

Sometimes it's relatively easy to construct a sample frame. If our population consists of Top 5 UK Law firm followers on Twitter, we could: 1) Identify top 5 UK law firms using publicly available lists, e.g. based on revenue data, 2) identify their Twitter accounts, and 3) identify those users on follower lists.

Some lists, that is sampling frames, are difficult, if not impossible to identify. For instance, how do you identify YouTube users aged 65 years and over?

If conducting a quantitative study, we could systematically search for demographic proxy measures to generate a list. This list would be incomplete and therefore risks sampling bias. Yet it's a realistic solution.

If undertaking a qualitative study, it's unlikely you will need a sampling frame in the first place! As highlighted next, sample selection in qualitative studies is guided by a different set of sampling criteria.

DEFINE YOUR SAMPLE

Unless working with big data, it is often impossible, impractical or undesirable to study a whole population. If we want to study UK Pinterest users, the population size will run into the millions. Instead we choose a sample of users (units) from our population of interest (X million Pinterest users) that we study (e.g. 50, 500, 1000 Pinterest users).

A PRE-DETERMINED SAMPLE SIZE NEEDED?

The sample size is the number of units we study. Whether we need to pre-determine our sample size will depend on our methodological approach.

Quantitative research seeks statistical generalizability. This involves calculating the optimal sample size. While this may prove too challenging, the general rule is that sample size is determined by the expected variation in the data. The more varied the data, the larger the sample size.

Qualitative research seeks analytical generalizability. Information richness, and often data saturation, is the goal. As such, in contrast to the pre-determined sampling steps taken in quantitative research, qualitative research takes a more flexible, iterative approach to sampling. Nonetheless, it's still important to consider how many people, cases or objects you may need to study.

BEWARE SAMPLING BIAS

Sampling bias refers to situations where the sample does not reflect the characteristics of our population of interest. Along with incomplete sampling frames, we also need to consider:

1   Self-selection bias – Inviting people to take part in our research study carries the risk that 'self-selected' participants could be different from our population of interest.

2   Coverage bias – Undercoverage bias occurs when population members do not appear in our sampling frame. Overcoverage bias occurs when there are duplicate records, for instance, retweets or multiple accounts.

Bias may also occur depending on our choice of sampling technique.

CHOOSING YOUR SAMPLING TECHNIQUE

When research is guided by a quantitative design, probabilistic sampling is best. Random sampling, systemic random sampling and stratified random sampling allow an equal chance (probability) that each unit (or units in each strata) in our population (N) could be selected for inclusion in our sample (n).

If random sampling is not possible, or qualitative research is chosen, non-probabilistic sampling is favoured. Convenience sampling involves selecting accessible people, cases or objects. While cheap and easy, it does lack rigour. Alternatively, judgement sampling, or purposive sampling, carefully selects cases from either a wide range, or extreme or special cases. Theoretical sampling is also possible, when our sampling is theory-driven. In this approach, we select more cases as our findings emerge to iteratively build theory.

HOW DO I CHOOSE MY SAMPLING TECHNIQUE

Choice of sampling technique is driven by your research question(s).

Quantitative enquiries are ideally placed to answer 'what?' and 'how much?' questions. And they are particularly apt for research that demands representativeness to enable generalization back to the population of interest.

In contrast, qualitative enquiries are particularly suited to 'how?' or 'why?' research questions. And despite all the excitement around big data, qualitative research can also deal with complex social problems. What's more, the threat of bias is often irrelevant, if people, cases or objects are selected due to their ability to illuminate a phenomenon in depth.

Fill in the Blanks

An effective social media sampling strategy produces ....
findings.

A sampling frame is a complete list of .... in
our population.

Name two types of sampling bias: i) ....
ii) ....

Simple random sampling is a .... sampling technique.

Convenience sampling is a .... sampling
technique.

Fill in the blanks in the following statements.

An effective social media sampling strategy produces _High quality_ findings.

A sampling frame is a complete list of _Units (of) Analysis_ in our population.

Name two types of sampling bias: i) _Self-selection_
ii) _Coverage_ .

Simple random sampling is a _Probabilistic_ sampling technique.

Convenience sampling is a _Non-probabilistic_ sampling technique.

Section

5

There are three
ways to extract
social media data

How do I extract data from social media platforms?

Depending on your research needs and know-how, social media data can be obtained in three different ways – via automated, manual or hybrid approaches.

Think before you extract

By now (or soon!) you will have a firm idea on what you are wanting to find out, what types of social media data you need, and from what and/ or whom you would like this data from. In this section, **you first need to consider how the social media data have been, or will be generated, before thinking through your query and data capture activities.**

How you extract data will depend on how it is generated.

Extant: Social media data that exists without any direct contact from the researcher. Examples could include forum discussions, social media posts, user interactions.

Elicited: Data that is directly elicited in response to a researcher's questions. Answers are elicited from people or non-human agents, such as chatbots.

DATA GENERATION TECHNIQUE

Enacted: Data that are enacted in collaboration with a researcher during an eventful study. This could involve social media messaging apps, simulation games and platform clones.

If data are elicited or enacted, it's likely your data will be manually extracted. However, if extant data are sought, you have several options.

Here are four important questions to ask to weigh up your options.

1 Data size – Does your research question demand big or small data?

2 Time – How much time do you have to collect your data?

3 Cost – Do free data collection methods fit the bill?

4 Know-how – Do you have the skills to collect your data?

BE REALISTIC

Manually collecting data is suitable for small *n* samples. Common practices include copying and pasting social media content and/or taking screenshots for subsequent analysis.

Extracting data manually is free and relatively easy to do. But it can be time-consuming and is prone to mistakes. For instance, if you accidentally miss a piece of data.

If you decide to extract data manually, keep manageability in mind.

EXTRACT BY
HAND

Automated data extraction involves collecting data with the help of computer programs. Researchers use platform public APIs to collect large n samples at relatively fast speeds. However, API access and use demand technical know-how and fluency in programming languages. This puts this option out of reach for many. Check platform developer sites to understand the challenges ahead.

Alternatively, third party providers offer data access from a wide range of platforms without the IT hassle. Yet they often carry a prohibitive fee. A few however do offer free plans, albeit with restricted data limits.

AUTOMATE YOUR EXTRACTIONS

You have several other options at your disposal.

Data repositories. An increasing number of online social media datasets are available for academic research. These could unlock relevant insights.

NCapture. This user-friendly free proprietary browser extension rapidly captures data from Facebook, Twitter, LinkedIn, YouTube and websites and can import up to tens of thousands of data records to Nvivo™.

COSMOS. The Social Data Science Lab's COSMOS software is available at no cost to academic institutions. While its data access is currently limited to Twitter's 1% data stream, it offers great tools to collect, mash and visualize social media data.

Mix it up. One collection method may not meet your research needs. You can mix elicited, extant and enacted data, and opt for a hybrid mix of manual and automated data collection methods.

EXPLORE ALL OPTIONS

We need to establish clear boundaries in data collection. Search criteria to query our research topic, or identify potential participants, will depend on our aims. Queries can use: keywords, hashtags, location, users, event names, timeframes, language or format (e.g. only retweets). Returned data can be structured (quantitative) and unstructured (qualitative). Seeking 'completeness' is the ideal, but here are some caveats to watch out for.

- Some terms are ambiguous. Try alternatives.

- People use different natural languages. Account for this.

- Not everyone will use your query terms. Search wider and deeper.

- Singular posts are only part of the story. Probe threads.

- Some topics defy the direct approach. Instead be creative, flexible and snowball when you hit gold.

DEFINE YOUR QUERY DESIGN

You can identify potential respondents for elicited or enacted studies during your query design. Alternatively, you can recruit offline, for instance face to face or via a university newspaper. Here are some ideas to formulate your recruitment strategy.

- Be prepared. Have your research questions ready before recruitment takes place.

- Produce a digitized or printed study information sheet and consent form to gain informed consent online or offline. Make sure these gain ethical approval before use.

- Invite directly (e.g. tweet invitation to potential participant), indirectly (e.g. broadcast your study (such as by posting in relevant, and ethically authorised places) or with help (e.g. via a forum moderator).

- Create a private list or online forum of (potential) participants for easy reference and research use.

WHEN RECRUITMENT IS REQUIRED

Get it?

Q: How do you avoid a 'garbage in, garbage out' data collection strategy?

Got it!

A: By giving careful consideration to the whole data collection process before getting your data.

SECTION

6

DIY: Take strategic steps to plan your data collection

What steps should I take to plan my data collection?

You need to flesh out the steps already covered to make sure you are clear on what your exciting research journey will involve.

Planning is everything!

Jumping in and getting social media data without a clear data collection plan is a recipe for mistakes. This DIY social media data collection plan section makes it far more likely you will conduct high-quality, ethical research that will reward you with valuable insights. It covers all sections of your data collection plan, with step-by-step explanations, examples and the space for you to write up your own notes.

Research Question/ Objectives

What to do:
Your data collection will be guided by your study's overarching research question and a set of focused objectives.

Step

1

EXAMPLE:

Research question:

How is climate change being framed by young Twitter and Instagram users in the UK?

Objectives:

To identify how climate change posts are being visually framed. To identify how climate change posts are being linguistically framed. To examine image-language interactions in the construction of social media frames.

YOUR TURN...

Jot down your research question and your objectives, making sure there is a logical link between them.

Research question:

. . . .
. . . .
. . . .
. . . .
. . . .
. . . .
. . . .
. . . .
. . . .
. . . .
. . . .

Research objectives:

. . . .
. . . .
. . . .
. . . .
. . . .
. . . .
. . . .
. . . .
. . . .
. . . .
. . . .
. . . .

Sampling Strategy

What to do:
This includes describing your population, sampling frame and sample as well as stating your sampling techniques.

2

EXAMPLE:

The population consists of social media posts generated by young people that contain climate change content on Twitter and Instagram. As a complete list of units of analysis within this population, i.e. the sampling frame, is beyond the reach of the researcher, a non-probabilistic convenience sample of 50 posts from each platform will be sought for this exploratory study. The main units of observation will be text, images and videos. Metadata will also be collected, including timestamp and location, where provided. User profiles in each sample will also be mined for geodemographic proxy measures – age and location information – to verify the sample posts have been generated by young people (18 to 25 years) living in the UK.

YOUR TURN...

Note down the key points of your sampling strategy.

Data Collection

What to do:
Describe how you will get your social media data. For instance, will you use a manual, automated or hybrid approach to data collection?

3

EXAMPLE:

Both Twitter and Instagram samples will be identified, by using each platform's search functionality. Searches will be made using climate change related hashtags e.g. #climatechange. Posts only making passing reference to climate change will be discarded. Posts that meet the sampling criteria will be extracted manually.

Be careful that your data collection is both ethical and manageable.

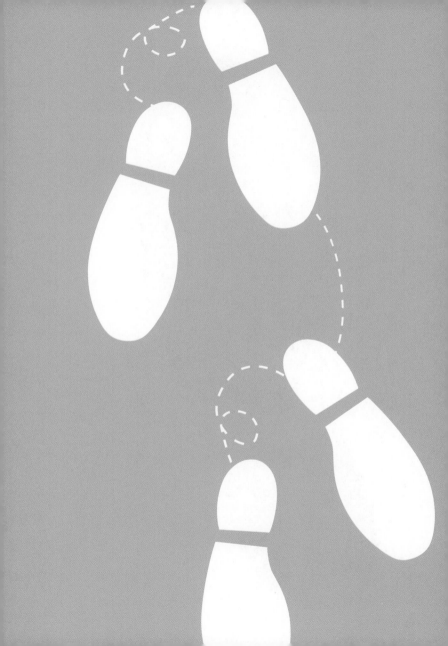

Research Ethics

What to do: State how your social media research meets your institution's ethical guidelines.

4

EXAMPLE:

Although the data available on Twitter and Instagram exist in the public domain, this study will follow our research ethics guidelines. The anonymity of all post authors will be protected, for instance their account ID and any reference to other account IDs (e.g. the use of @) will be removed. To avoid the use of data generated by potentially vulnerable people, only posts that can be verified as that generated by authors aged 18 or above, will be used for research purposes. Both raw and coded data will be stored for two years on password-protected files on a password-protected computer. As this research is for education purposes only, the study will not be made public to ensure both anonymity and confidentiality.

YOUR TURN...

Double check your research will meet your institution's ethics guidelines.

CONGRATULATIONS!

YOU'VE GOT A PLAN TO GET YOUR SOCIAL MEDIA DATA!

Work through this checklist to help ensure you have mastered all you need to know to get your data from social media.

☐ Do you understand the value and limitations of using social media data? If not, go back to p. 9.

☐ Do you understand the necessary steps to conduct your social media research to high ethical standards? If not, go back to p. 27.

☐ Are you able to identify the type and scope of data you are intending to collect? If not, go back to p. 47.

HOW TO KNOW YOU ARE DONE

☐ Have you got to grips with the different elements of an effective sampling strategy? If not, go back to p. 69.

☐ Are you able to collect data, manually and/or via computer assistance, to meet your research needs? If not, go back to p. 87.

☐ Have you completed the steps needed to plan your social media research? If not, go back to p. 103.

Glossary

Application programming interface (API) Social media platforms provide a window to developers to allow platform and data access.

Big data This refers to the huge volume of data – structured and unstructured – generated by social media. It also describes the field that uses computational methods to extract meaning from this data.

Chatbot An artificially intelligent software that can simulate a conversation with a user.

Content analysis This involves the analysis of social media content either by counting (quantitative) and/or coding (qualitative) to extract meaning.

Data mining This describes data discovery methods to find hidden patterns in large volumes of data.

Discourse analysis This analysis goes 'beyond the sentence', and can analyse context, structure, form, organization and patterns as well as the dynamic aspects of discourse, including social interactions.

Geomask A technique to protect privacy but still allow a valid analysis of geographic data.

Geotag A digital tag that assigns a geographic location to a piece of data, for instance a photograph, video or post.

Metadata This is data that describes another set of data. This could refer to structured data assigned to user accounts and posts or a machine-readable description of a whole dataset.

Natural Language Processing This analytical technique involves computer-aided processing and analysis of large amounts of natural language data.

Netnography   This online research method is grounded in ethnographic principles and involves the observation of social interactions in online and social media environments.

Online ethnography   This methodology involves any ethnography study in digital and online environments, but does not do so exclusively, as its research approach may extend to the offline world as well.

Online focus group   This research method is where a small group of participants can share and debate a topic in a virtual environment.

Social bot   This is a non-human agent that chats and interacts in an autonomous manner in online environments.

Social Network Analysis   SNA can measure and map the networked relationships and flows between people, organizations and objects.

Unit of analysis   The 'who' or the 'what' you want to study. The unit of analysis will likely be people – consumers, voters, patients and so on – or cases – organizations, brands, political parties, cities, or objects – hashtags, posts, fan pages, platforms.

Unit of observation   A unit of observation is the data you will observe, measure or collect to understand your unit of analysis. If your unit of analysis is a person, your units of observation could be feelings, thoughts and behaviours.

Visual analytics   The science of analytical reasoning facilitated by interactive visual interfaces.